THE JOY OF LEARNING

THE JOY OF LEARNING

Unlocking Your Intellectual Potential

ELIAS HARTLEY

QuillQuest Publishers

CONTENTS

Copyright © 2024 by Elias Hartley

All rights reserved. No part of this book may be reproduced in any manner whatsoever without written permission except in the case of brief quotations embodied in critical articles and reviews.

First Printing, 2024

CHAPTER 1

Introduction

At every stage of life, the potential for lifelong learning continues to amaze. Every new experience, every new challenge, every useful failure is a potential curriculum for deeper insight and understanding, for not just more knowledge and better skills, but for the delight that comes when one's understanding reaches well beyond the original boundaries of the task. The remarkable thing is that learning itself, done well, can be its own reward.

Of course, learning is not always a simple task. It is a complex and somewhat unpredictable process that changes as we age. It follows its own rules, and it is as unique as the individual seeking to learn. The purpose of this text is to explore the nature of the learning process and the reasoning, thinking, and practicing choices that lead to powerful, higher-level learning - and to explore these processes in the context of both the potential and the limitations of the human mind. It is concerned not just about learning in the narrow context of formal education, but about learning throughout life. It examines the issues of what to learn, what one brings to the learning effort, and how best to learn. The reader should find many points of comparison with the way one currently learns or teaches, suggestions for improvement, and hopefully, a greater sense of confidence or even joy in the learning process itself.

Understanding the Value of Lifelong Learning

It is urgent because we need the spontaneous rush of curiosity - in some it is insatiable - to make up more of the levers that think. Ignorance is contagious, as we happen to be learning from two scourges - illness and unenlightenment - that were supposed to be on their way out. Lifelong learning is no longer a casual leisure activity, enjoyed in the breather between employment and retirement. Rather it is an integral but undeclared part of the employment/retirement process itself. The word that best captures the essence of the twenty-first century, however, is 'freelance'. I am especially pleased to be able to propose a reevaluation of the excellence of those intangible qualities and abilities that our alumni acquire at a stage in their life when they lack specialized knowledge and methods but possess a more valuable treasure: the capacity for vision, the enthusiasm of change, and the ability to communicate.

Our schools, from kindergarten all the way to the universities, are terrific. And they do a terrific job, on the whole. The problem is, there's not enough of them. Not enough schools, not enough teachers, and above all not enough excitement in the act of learning. Those young people who are ravenously curious, interested in everything, come to be seen as freaks and marginalized, when they are in fact the only truly educable spirits. Good teachers can hold a whole class's attention, filling everyone with wonder or excitement. But these teachers are almost as rare as the students who want to be thrust with a burning desire to know. Unfortunately, even if we had enough classes and enough dedicated teachers, it would still not be enough. We have to fix the appetite for learning, and to do this at both ends of the life cycle. That is just as urgent and just as difficult as building more schools and training more teachers.

CHAPTER 2

Part I: Foundations of Learning

Ah, how sociology would benefit! Ah, how economics would be enriched. Human capital would be measured and laissez-faire could be applied to the educational system. It is not possible to go directly to the vast field of human understanding. Allow me an off-trail... preparedStatement as it is. All I dare to do is to present this little piece of the immensity that is the human thirst for learning. Education is a calling, a very specialized human activity. The school is a privileged place for the pursuit of knowledge with an established, albeit nascent curriculum. Teaching is a craft and a true art. It is not by chance that eternity accompanies learning adorns some of the oldest universities. I declare myself a zealous advocate of the formal education of children, prioritizing attention, dedication, and love. And progress is more than necessary. But I do not commit the error of ignoring informal education. It is through it that parents work marvels and through it that we learn the most fascinating hobbies.

First and foremost, in our examination of the sources of joy in learning, we begin with the tool of learning: the instrument with which we master reality. This tool is our mind, the great subject of cognitive science in our day. There are and there will be so many questions to be addressed regarding human learning, evidence, models, artificial intelligence, heuristics and biases, schemas and networks, resources in long-term memory, forgetting and memory, motivation and curiosity. But the basic question remains the same as four centuries ago: "What a piece of work is man?... And yet, to me, what is this quintessence of dust?" We have now constructed machines that seem better than ourselves at doing the tasks we have been describing. We have calculated new ways of computing that are even better than the silicon ones. But we do not understand more now than before what it is that makes us capable of understanding.

The Science of Learning

Given the potential improvement in education possible through directed effort, this book attempts to package disparate psychological, educational, and recently developed neurological knowledge into a coherent whole. More importantly, it aims to operationalize the vague suggestions created by these fields into concrete, everyday practice. This will allow you not only to vastly improve your own core skills at learning, since this whole model will allow you to create detailed plans and schedules for continuous recursive practice and improvement, but it will also allow you to continuously and deliberately hone the intellectual potential of others.

Unfortunately, these approaches have yet to be implemented on a wide scale, and only the most motivated self-learners tend to pull any scientific knowledge in. This oversight highlights what will be a driving theme of this book: that learning, like the world, is highly fractal, with successful mental strategies translatable over a vast range of scales and subjects. Yet, such strategies remain largely implicit and inaccessible for many of our brightest scholars. This implicitness limits the success of even the most talented individuals, and in these days, the pace of learning quickly pulls many of the luminaries pulled from school into obscurity. Further, this relative dearth of knowledge implicitly penalizes youth, as students unaware of these tools do not possess them and likely burn out in a premature attempt to collect them.

Scientific ways to improve how we learn are nothing new. Scientists have been studying ways to improve metacognition and both general and domain-specific skill development for over a century, and some form of educational science has been around in the US since at least 1867. Psychologists, neuroscientists, anthropologists, linguists, and educators continue to make significant contributions, creating both a well-honed base of knowledge and skills in instructional design and the psychology of learners. Occasionally, schools discard more effective techniques, such as timely, conceptual feedback in some of the material within major courses in which students regularly struggle.

CHAPTER 3

Part II: Cultivating a Growth Mindset

When we better understand the brain's potential and limitations, we can adjust our expectations, letting ourselves off the hook a bit more and focusing our efforts on creating the mental connections that will help us learn efficiently. The growth mindset, in short, is appreciating and understanding our brain's remarkable characteristics, using them to our advantage.

We're often our worst critics because we expect our brains to quickly understand complicated concepts, then master them just as fast. We forget that the brain is unique, but that doesn't mean the brain's limitations will hold us hostage. Instead, we can work with the brain's shortcomings and capitalize on its unique strengths and abilities.

Our brain's ability to grow and change is hardwired into its core. Our brains are made of humble cells that connect or 'wire' with each other, called neurons. We have about 80 billion neurons, but what's unique is that they can form new connections or new 'wiring'. This means that with each new bit of information we learn, experience we have, or memory we form, we're creating new synapses or neurons that wire together.

What is a growth mindset? It's a belief that our talents and abilities can be developed through dedicated effort, deliberate practice, and constructive feedback. This belief is essential for helping you maximize your intellectual growth. Let's dive into our first growth mindset principle: a deeper understanding of the brain's malleability.

Embracing Challenges

The key factor seems to be the degree to which a person believes in being able to influence events. This is the person's locus of control. People who have a high internal locus of control believe that events and personal outcomes are largely governed by their own actions and decisions, while people who have a high external locus of control believe that events and personal outcomes are greatly impacted by life's vicissitudes: other people, fate, luck, and destiny. In some respects, people with an internal locus of control are intellectually tougher than people with an external locus of control: They display greater persistence in the face of obstacles, they tend to try harder to master a problem, to work more effectively and efficiently, and they show greater resistance to despair. So it is a higher internal locus of control that encourages people to participate in new learning experiences with enthusiasm and to perform with optimal effectiveness. The reason people with an external locus of control shy away from challenges isn't because they are afraid of failure—after all, people with an internal locus of control experience failure too—it's because they simply don't see themselves in the driver's seat. They don't expect to succeed, so they don't even bother to try. Simply standing up to every learning challenge you face is the hallmark of the successful, highly self-efficacious people in the world. It is the attitude, above all, that distinguishes people who seem to master almost anything.

Imagine that we are endowed with a certain amount of intellectual firepower at birth. Many people, however, don't exercise full command of that firepower. When they are confronted with a difficult problem, do they rise to the challenge or do they simply give up? Many people, unfortunately, give up. Of course, they don't just roll over and die; they do indeed solve an obstacle on their way to learning a foreign language, they do come up with a tentative solution to a physics problem. Yes, but they do so at the expense of their intellectual power. They do not let their natural gifts shine. They let the muscles of their intellectual minds atrophy rather than develop them to a dazzling form. Now why is this? You might guess that people shy away from challenges because they are lazy, but studies indicate that laziness itself doesn't account for this phenomenon.

CHAPTER 4

Part III: Effective Learning Strategies

Many effective learning techniques have been uncovered, and the reader will note that not all have been included in this book. I have prepared a short list of other effective learners, which follows. Although hardly comprehensive, the list gives readers a brief introduction to some additional but important learning tools. The reader is urged to study them at least briefly because he may find their ideas both intriguing and practical.

The study techniques described in the preceding chapters are among the most powerful learning tools developed by scientists interested in human learning and memory. The mnemonic strategies have been used effectively for many centuries, but the discovery of the basic cognitive and physiological factors which contribute to their success is very recent. During the 20th century, scientists also discovered that many processing mechanisms involved in learning enhance thermal efficiency - but only when they are used voluntarily.

Active Learning Techniques

Many methodologies are available that deliberately involve students in the learning process. Learning tools that depend more on personal critical thinking and less on rote learning help to ensure better retention of the information presented. Among these strategies, one of the most important is the use of small groups. The ability to interact is key. A warm class atmosphere in which there is questioning during a lecture, and ready response to questions by the teacher and student, can be as effective as small group activities. Any technique which permits interaction among students on an individual basis is generally helpful. The more informal the interactions, the easier it is to get involved, the more powerful the learning.

One strategy that is particularly effective in ensuring active learning involves repeating the material: reading it, hearing it in a lecture, discussing it in small groups with others and writing on it in daily journals or lab reports, and so forth. These diverse activities use different ways to reinforce learning so that the substance of the material is more likely to be remembered after the class is over. Especially in a large class where there is a tendency to skim the surface of material without any personal understanding or in a class where most of the time is spent listening to lectures, such small group or in-class discussions, debates, problem-solving, collaboration with the instructor, and other forms of active learning are most important to the enjoyment of learning.

CHAPTER 5

Part IV: Overcoming Learning Barriers

Learning coexists with an intruding background of disabling influence of living and learning in an educational milieu that has configured itself, in order to, detached from the real world it pretends to serve. Many of the barriers to learning are 'learned' during your school years! When any mentioned deficiencies have their "cognitive-cultural" origins in society, it is the corresponding society's responsibility to redress the resultant educational disadvantages. But who or what should shoulder the responsibility of training individuals to becoming better learners and comprehenders? It will have to be the society itself. The development of a learning society is a responsibility of the society, a natural law of development, much needed.

The ability to learn is natural; learning with joy is its ultimate outcome. But often, learning may be impeded - blocked by barriers that the learner has unwittingly imposed. This part deals with these barriers and offers suggestions to overcome them. Exercise in critical thinking is one of these. Done as sport and open pursuit of meaning, critical thinking is a basic burden you bear to ensure the quality of your learning. So true it is that it is difficult to imagine the intellectual survival of the newly-independent citizens of a free breeding society without a concurrent flowering of critical thinking, as well as all the rites of citizenship.

Procrastination and Perfectionism

Socrates mentioned to one of his students that he objected to the practice which some of the teachers had, who were always harping the parnassian precepts that had been delivered by others, when they ought rather to search for truth themselves and not be always repeating what had already been uttered. This is better, said he, not to find your mistake in matters of small importance; for, standing words, with whom I cannot endure to treat idle disputes, I am in some doubt whether deception of these is, on the whole, so dangerous as that of others, as I find nothing so pernicious in the view as mere wordiness.

In the previous chapter, we talked about the importance of motivation in overcoming educational obstacles and gave some tips for creating and sustaining it. In this chapter, we will address some specific types of problems that may arise in connection with motivation. These include many common difficulties that people have with intellectual work, such as procrastination and perfectionism. If you find yourself experiencing some of these difficulties, we hope you will be comforted and encouraged by the following discussion.

CHAPTER 6

Part V: Applying Your Learning

Of course, the trick is to avoid the package of disappointment so many of us carry around, which is that if something worked its way into our minds, we shouldn't have to stick it there again by reviewing. If we need to study a set of flashcards or read over a chapter, then something is wrong. Didn't we pay our dues? Didn't we already do whatever is necessary to show up for understanding? If we understand it well, shouldn't these things be irrelevant? If we don't understand it, then is it worth understanding? This attitude overlooks the basic facts about how our minds work and the extraordinary efficiency of cognitive apprenticeship. If you are becoming a chef, you slice a carrot, then go on to clean a pot, then put a pot of water on the stove to boil, then slice a rutabaga—the instructor arranges a sequence that is somewhat like what you will one day have to do as a chef. Then the instructor begins to vary the sequence, breaking routines and throwing new complications in. Soon enough, you are flambéing bananas, and you have no trouble; you have learned how to enter yourself in everything you've done. The sequence is all. The craft is so unlike the way one lives through it that it would overlap functionally with those very things that one assumes a study group is trying to prepare...

As you finish this book, I want to offer you one more word about where learning goes awry—because many people have a fallacious strategy for school, which stems from disappointment that they think of as lifelong learning, and it is altogether unnecessary. It may even make the insatiable joy of learning seem sour and like hard work. I direct your attention to the title of this chapter: "One More Time." This simple phrase captures an absolutely essential way in which the human mind works, as the scholar Hermann Ebbinghaus discovered in the 1880s. Our memory for things is greatly enhanced by reexposure. Present to a student a point about, say, Roman history in a reading, a lecture, a discussion, and you may or may not generate a little learning. But if that same date and event turn up unexpectedly in a conversation the next week, then rearrange the kids' soccer games, your message enters long-term memory: "Oh, yeah," the student says, "A.D. 14, that's when Augustus died. We talked about that in class. I remember now."

Interdisciplinary Thinking

All of us are only a lifetime away from Plato and Aristotle. But the demands of interdisciplinary thinking are many, and they must be met with precision. First, make sure that you are interested in everything. Then, examine your own unique library. Look at your study habits. The human brain can retain very little data. It performs searches for data that describe an experience only in response to a query. If the query doesn't come, no search is made. Nothing is learned. The brain does search repositories quite frequently. The normal life process is one of managing personal experience in databases. Discussions with other individuals are the only experiences that are completely spontaneous. The LTS stress the need for at least some of these experiences to be disciplined and scheduled, and the resulting discussion can contribute to constructing the queries.

Many people say that they are interested in everything. Only a few really are – in the sense that they can take a lifelong formal interest in everything and learn how to learn almost any subject. To do this, the student must be consciously interdisciplinary. To anyone intrigued by the beauty of learning, one discipline – even the arts – is simply not enough. It dwarfs the boundary between universality and technicality and takes up its place beside the classical languages, history, philosophy, and the study of religion as a necessary foundation for interdisciplinary thinking. Just as language is linked to literature, music to tone, studies of human relationships to ethics, and academic studies to philosophy and theology, economics, the study of how individuals and societies cope with scarcity, is linked to psychology, human desires, and their fulfillment or frustration.

CHAPTER 7

Conclusion

Our aim, in a nutshell, is to help you become an autodidact, hopefully for life, not for a specific period in your education. Whatever strategy you currently espouse, the next big step forward is for it to be of your own making, for a set of learning techniques that you develop and evolve in the light of your own experience. Once you take that step, you'll discover that the joy of learning is not only within your reach, but very much exactly what is meant by discovering who you truly are.

We conclude where we began, with the essential question of whether or not learning can indeed bring joy. The answer can only be yes, learning can bring you endless joy when you feel the immediacy and intrinsic rewards of interrogating the world around you with your intellect. If, thus freed and spurred on by passion and intrinsic motivation, you click with the right technique, then your learning will be fast, effective, deeply satisfying and qualitatively different from what you know now. It will also be 'future proof', because the techniques you use will equip you to continue to acquire new knowledge throughout your life. And the learning techniques that endure will be those that focus on cognitive activities.

Sustaining Your Passion for Learning

Strategy 1: Cultivate flexibility, humility, and humor. As we take our intellectual journey throughout life, we need to constantly adjust our goals, our perspectives, and our behavior. Seeing clearly in the present to prepare for the future requires flexibility, an openness to new ideas, and the humility to draw on others with different perspectives and types of expertise. Always be ready to change your mind. Look for the sustainable principles in concepts that are offered to you; be humble and appreciative of the perspectives and expertise of others; and cultivate an appreciation of paradoxes. Without humility, flexibility, and humor, the "free radical" that is pursuing mastery will probably end up being more rascal than freethinker.

There are only two forces of potential change that are within our control when it comes to ourselves: the lives we choose to lead and how we grow in our hearts and our minds. Choosing to learn and grow in areas that light our fires is a realizable lifelong objective. Enjoy your journey into the realms of lifelong learning.

Concluding comments. It is my sincere hope that the strategies I have outlined in this book will help you to lead a life of joyful discovery. Since we have come to the end of our journey, we may find it useful to reflect for a moment on how you can sustain your passion for learning and maintain your will to grow. Here are seven ingredients for a life of intellectual bliss: Keep growing personally. Grow within yourself. Live by your principles and be true to yourself. Always be designing your future, and live in the present as you create your future blueprint. Cultivate flexibility, humility, and humor. Always be sifting, and become adept at seeing phenomena from different points of view. Draw stimulation and support from others. Build an environment that encourages and rewards learning. Become an expert in some area of knowledge. Immerse yourself in a single domain of knowledge. Be a little unique in this domain, because the only uniqueness that has any real lasting value is uniqueness that exists within a domain of expertise.

www.ingramcontent.com/pod-product-compliance
Lightning Source LLC
Chambersburg PA
CBHW051411130726
47987CB00007B/2951